Module 2 • Set 1 • Creature Code

CONTENTS

This book belongs to

. . . .

GREAT MINDS

Great Minds® is the creator of *Eureka Math®*, *Wit & Wisdom®*, *Alexandria Plan™*, and *PhD Science™*.

Geodes® are published by Great Minds in association with Wilson Language Training, publisher of *Fundations®*.

Credits

- *Vervet Monkey Alarm*: folio icon, Aratehortua/Shutterstock.com; About the Animals page (top), Martin Mecnarowski/Shutterstock.com, (second from top), Joe McDonald/Shutterstock.com, (third from top), Matthieu Gallet/Shutterstock.com, (bottom), Robert Wedderburn/Shutterstock.com; More page, Christopher Reusch/Shutterstock.com

- *Smell Tells*: front cover and pp. 12–13, RusticBoy/Shutterstock.com; folio icon, Brian Goff/Shutterstock.com; p. 1, Wiratchai Wansamngam/Shutterstock.com; p. 2 and back cover, Andrey Pavlov/Shutterstock.com; p. 3, (top), Pan Xunbin/Shutterstock.com; (bottom), irin-k/Shutterstock.com; p. 4, ta'/Moment Open/Getty Images; p. 5, alybaba/Shutterstock.com; pp. 6–7, Susan Thompson Photography/Moment/Getty Images; pp. 8–9, iStock.com/KonArt; p. 9 (black ant), Africa Studio/Shutterstock.com; pp. 10–11 (top), Paul Taylor/Photodisc/Getty Images; p. 11 (bottom), arlindo71/E+/Getty Images; p. 14, Yutthapong Rassamee/Shutterstock.com; More page, Erik T. Frank

- *Bee Waggle*: More page, photo by rtbilder/Shutterstock.com

- *Elephant Talk*: front cover, Johan Swanepoel/Shutterstock.com; title page and p. 7, Nature Picture Library/Alamy Stock Photo; p. 1 (left), Katja Forster/Shutterstock.com, (right), Matthieu Gallet/Shutterstock.com; p. 2, Paula French/Shutterstock.com; p. 3, clickit/Shutterstock.com; pp. 4–5, ElephantVoices, www.elephantvoices.org; p. 6, Jeffrey B. Banke/Shutterstock.com; p. 9, robertharding/Alamy Stock Photo; pp. 10–11, Matej Kastelic/Shutterstock.com; p. 12, Charlotte Raboff/Shutterstock.com; p. 13, John Carnemolla/Shutterstock.com; p. 14, Anup Shah/Minden Pictures/Getty Images; More page, Michael K. McDermott/Shutterstock.com; back cover, Peter Betts/Shutterstock.com

VERVET MONKEY ALARM

EMILY GULA
GIULIANO FERRI

I have lots to do.

I hang. I nap. I eat. I play.

I spy.

Why do I spy?

I have to protect my group.

Come! Be a spy with me.

I see it.

Can you?

We are not safe

with him here.

3

I yell, *"RUFF, RUFF!"*

This tells them to run
up the tree.

We swing from the top.

He can not get us here.

Yes! We are safe.

Oh no.

I see it.

Can you?

We are not safe

with her here.

I yell, *"ROP, ROP!"*
This tells them
to dash down.

We sink into the shrub.
She can not get us here.
Yes! We are safe.

Oh no.

I see it.

Can you?

We are not safe

with him here.

I yell,

"CHAT, CHAT!"

This tells them
to stand up.

We form a ring.

There is a gang of us.

There is one of him.

It does not take long.

He is gone.

"Ssss," says he.

"Too many monkeys for me."

ABOUT THE ANIMALS

vervet monkey

leopard

eagle

python

MORE

More than 30 years ago, scientists spent 14 months observing vervet monkeys in Kenya. They noted how the vervets made different sounds when a predator, such as a leopard or snake, approached. When other members of the monkey troop heard the call, they moved away from the predator. The scientists noticed this movement. They wondered if the monkeys were responding to the call or if they also saw the predator.

To learn more, the scientists planned an experiment. First, they recorded monkey calls when a predator came close to the troop. Later, when the scientists knew there was no predator nearby, they used a hidden speaker to play a call. Through repeated observation, the scientists found that the monkeys moved to different spots based on the call.

Scientists discover more with each new study. They learn how animals communicate and survive.

MÁS

Hace más de 30 años, unos científicos pasaron 14 meses observando a los monos vervet en Kenia. Observaron cómo hacían diversos sonidos cuando algunos depredadores, como el leopoardo o la víbora, se acercaban. Cuando otros miembros de la manada oían el llamado, estos alejaban del depredador. Los científicos advirtieron este movimiento. Se preguntaron si los monos respondían al llamado o si también veían el depredador.

Para saber más, los científicos planearon un experimento. Primero, grabaron los llamados de los monos cuando un depredador se acercaba a la manada. Después, cuando los científicos sabían que no había ningún depredador cerca, escondieron un altavoz para reproducir el llamado. Mediante observaciones repetidas, los científicos descubrieron que los monos se movían hacia diferentes puntos según el llamado.

Los científicos descubren algo nuevo con cada estudio. Aprenden cómo se comunican y sobreviven los animales.

Smell Tells

Mamie Goodson

One whiff
can tell a *lot*.

An ant has two
long antennae.

With the tips of them,
it can smell very well.

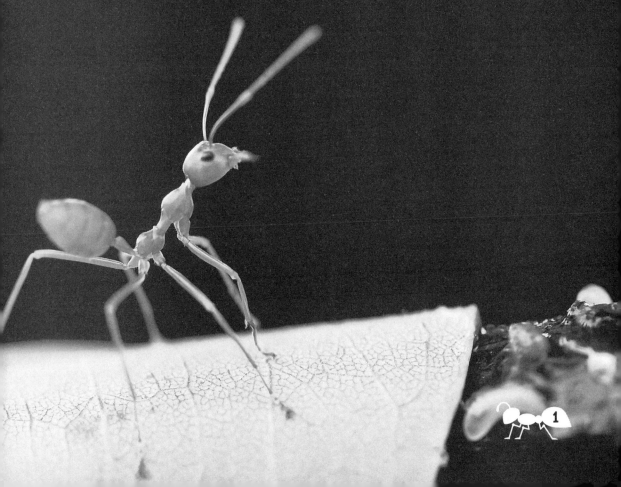

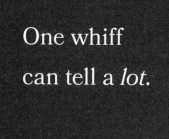

1

Smell tells who is who.

Two ants meet.

Pat, pat, pat.

They can tell rank.

This one is a queen.

This one is a worker.

They can tell

one of the gang

with a whiff.

Smell tells where to find food.

This ant finds
a hunk of rich food.
She nips at a chunk
and then runs
back to the nest.

4

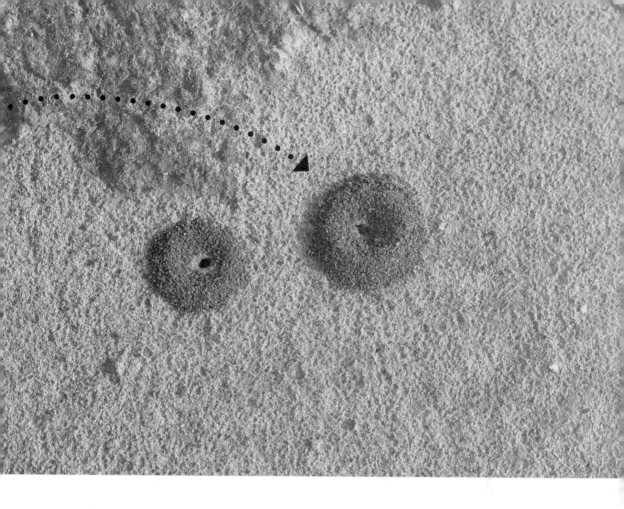

As she runs back,
she sets up a path
they can smell.
This is a map
for the gang.

6

They set off
on the path,
one by one.

They find
that chunk of food, too.
It is a win
for the gang!

Smell tells how to be safe.

This ant is in danger!
She lets off a scent.
It tells pals:
"Come quick!"

This nest is not safe!

She packs up the gang.

She sets up a path

they can smell.

They rush off
to a safe hill.

11

One whiff
can tell a lot
to an ant.

13

Smell lets ants
live and work
as one big group.

More

There are more than 10,000 species of ants in the world. They live on every continent except Antarctica.

No matter where they live, ants form colonies. Within these groups, worker ants have different jobs. Sometimes an ant hunts for food; other times it tends the nest.

Worker ants in one African species sometimes help injured nestmates, too. The wounded ant releases a scent called a pheromone. The smell tells any nearby ant to come to the rescue. The rescuer ant then carries the injured ant back to the nest, where it can recover.

Más

Existen más de 10,000 especies de hormigas en el mundo. Viven en todos los continentes, excepto en la Antártida.

Independientemente de dónde vivan, las hormigas forman colonias. En estos grupos las hormigas trabajadoras tienen diferentes funciones. A veces una hormiga busca comida; otras veces cuida el nido.

Las hormigas trabajadoras de una de las especies africanas a veces ayudan a sus compañeras de nido cuando están heridas. La hormiga herida libera un aroma llamado feromona. Ese aroma avisa a otra hormiga que esté cerca que debe ir a su rescate. La hormiga que va al rescate carga a la otra hasta el nido para que se recupere.

Bee Waggle

Catherine Schmidt   Christopher Cyr

Bees do a jig.

They kick and they bob.

Why do they do this?

It's part of the job!

The worker bee bops
and bats a wing.
The jig helps the group
to find one thing.

She zips to the hive.

There's a buzz in the shack.

3

Come here! Come quick!

There is dust on her back.

Can the group find the food?

She steps to the rink.

"Observe my dance,"

she tells with a wink.

The food is far,

so the dash is long.

She kicks and she bops.

They sing a buzz song.

Her wag tells where.

The jig is a map.
To get to the nectar,

they study the tap.

9

Then one by one,
off the bees zing.
They follow the map
to find the rich thing!

Safe in the hive,
some bees hang back.
They mix up the honey.
They add to the stack.

Bees cut a rug.

They jig and they bob.

To make the honey,

they all do a job.

More

Karl von Frisch spent more than 40 years studying bees. He discovered how bees use movement to communicate. Von Frisch called these movements dances. For his work, von Frisch won a Nobel Prize.

Through observation, von Frisch identified how bees use two moves to communicate a flower's location. The first move gives clues about distance. Bees waggle a longer time to show that a flower is farther away. The second move points to the flower's direction.

Once a dance is completed, the bees go in search of the flower. The flower provides the nectar the hive will use to produce honey. Bees must visit two million flowers to collect enough nectar to make just one pound of honey.

Más

Karl von Frisch se dedicó durante más de 40 años a estudiar las abejas. Descubrió cómo las abejas usan el movimiento para comunicarse. Von Frisch les llamó bailes a estos movimientos. Von Frisch ganó el Premio Nobel por su trabajo.

Por medio de la observación von Frisch identificó cómo las abejas usan dos movimientos para comunicar la ubicación de una flor. El primer movimiento indica la distancia. Las abejas se menean durante más tiempo para indicar que una flor está más lejos. El segundo movimiento apunta en la dirección de la flor.

Una vez que el baile ha terminado, las abejas salen en busca de la flor. La flor les da el néctar que el panal utilizará para producir miel. Las abejas deben visitar dos millones de flores para recoger suficiente néctar para producir tan solo una libra de miel.

ELEPHANT TALK

written by Catherine Schmidt

Elephants have a lot to tell.

They do it with no words at all.

They call to tell.

They smell to tell.

They move big ears,

trunks,

and legs

to tell things to the group.

She trumpets with her long trunk.

It tells them:

"Let's get together."

They hear the call.

They jog to her.

Mom is boss.

She jabs one big leg.

She hums and rumbles.

It tells them:

"Let's go this way."

They hear the hum.

They line up.

He finds some dung.

Who put it there?

With one whiff,

the smell tells him:

"It's from a pal."

There's the pal.

The dung was his!

He puts up his trunk.

He takes a whiff.

A smell can tell who is here.

If it is a lion,

they will run.

He tells the gang:

"It is not a big cat."

It's safe.

They do not run.

MOVES CAN TELL

She rumbles.

She bangs one big foot.

The herd is in danger.

Far off, the big thud tells them:

"Look out!"

They feel the thud and buzz in their legs.

They protect the calf.

The gang is here.

The group is back.

Some rub and hum.

Some kick and honk.

It is a celebration.

It tells them:

"This is a happy group!"

This gang has a lot to tell.

They talk with no words at all.

More

Elephants use their mouths, tongues, trunks, and more to produce many sounds. These sounds range from low rumbles to high-pitched trumpets. The noises that come out of an elephant's mouth sound different from those that travel through its trunk. The trunk sounds are louder or deeper. An elephant can change those sounds further by widening its nostrils.

Elephants have another unique feature for communicating. An elephant has a pouch behind its tongue. The muscles inside this pouch move, or vibrate, to make very low sounds. Many of these sounds are so low that humans cannot hear them. It is estimated that humans can hear fewer than half the sounds elephants produce.

Más

Los elefantes usan sus bocas, lenguas, trompas, y otras partes de su cuerpo para producir muchos sonidos. Estos van desde sonidos muy bajos hasta barritos agudos. Los sonidos que provienen de la boca del elefante son diferentes de los que recorren su trompa. Los sonidos de la trompa son más fuertes o más graves. Un elefante puede modificar esos sonidos al ensanchar las fosas nasales.

Los elefantes tienen otra característica única que les permite comunicarse. Tienen una bolsa detrás de la lengua. Los músculos dentro de esta bolsa se mueven, o vibran, para producir sonidos muy bajos. Muchos de estos sonidos son tan bajos que los seres humanos no pueden oírlos. Se calcula que los seres humanos pueden oír menos de la mitad de los sonidos que producen los elefantes.